NO

Made for Music

ELTON JOHN

STEVIE WONDER

JOHN DENVER

Made for Music

ELTON JOHN
STEVIE WONDER
JOHN DENVER

by George Zanderbergen

Published by Crestwood House, Inc., Mankato Minnesota 56001. Published simultaneously in Canada by J.M. Dent and Sons, Ltd. Printed in the United States of America.

Library of Congress Catalog Card Number: 76-24208. International Standard Book Number: 0-913940-51-8.

Design - Doris Woods and Randal M. Heise

PHOTOGRAPHIC CREDITS

The illustration of this book was made possible through the cooperation of:

John Reid Enterprises for Elton John, Wide World Photo's, Wortoke Concern Inc. public relations for Stevie Wonder, Mark Ahlstrom, United Press International.

Made for Music

ELTON JOHN

STEVIE WONDER

JOHN DENVER

Elton John

You see him on the stage. He is dressed in a fantastic costume that may have cost thousands of dollars. His eyeglass frames wink with jewels. As changing colored lights flash around him, he plays the piano and sings.

Stubby fingers pound out chords with a steady beat — beat — beat, like a heart-throb. The song is "Someone Saved My Life Tonight."

Everyone listens to the sad lyrics. The person in the song has loved unwisely. He has nearly been tied down. He has escaped his love, only to discover that this is painful, too. He gives in to depression, but someone saves him. Newly wise, he realizes that he is a butterfly. He must be free to love and then fly away.

The song ends on a plaintive note. The audience cheers. And Elton John, the gaudy butterfly of rock music, accepts the applause.

The song, like many others that Elton has written, reflects a part of his own life. He has been unhappy, he has despaired and tried to take his life. He has been saved by friends. He has looked into his own heart and come to terms with the person that he is.

And he sings about it.

His fantastic costumes hide a body that is short and slight. His near-sighted eyes are masked behind glasses trimmed with fur, feathers, beads, or diamonds. He seems to say, "I am an ordinary person — but not really! Inside I glitter and gleam. I sparkle and change color. Which butterfly shape is me? Pick the one you like best — but you still won't know the real me."

Some of his songs are pure hard rock. Others have a country song. There are deep songs such as "Rocket Man" and "Daniel." There are ballads. There are middle-of-the-road songs. Pick the one you like best! They are all part of Elton John.

Who is the real Elton John?

When the concert is over, he takes off his flashy costume. Then he is a slight, 29-year-old man who wouldn't stand out in a crowd. He has a shy smile. He's going a little bald. He is somewhat embarrassed when people remind him that he's a multi-millionaire.

The real Elton John is a man who lives for music. He writes songs quickly — usually putting music to words composed by his friend, Bernie Taupin. He says he doesn't take the songs seriously. (But if that's true, why are so many of them obviously about him?)

He likes to kid his image as a rock superstar. "People shouldn't take the clothes so seriously," he says. "Honestly, it's just a joke. Just a good-natured way of sending up the rock'n'roll business by saying: 'Here it is! Let's all have a laugh and enjoy ourselves.' "

Elton John says he didn't begin to enjoy himself until he was 21 years old.

He was born in 1947 in Pinner, England, the only child of Stanley and Sheila Dwight. His name was Reginald Kenneth Dwight. Stanley was a squadron leader in the Royal Air Force. He spent a lot of time away from home.

Little Reggie's mother was a gentle, loving woman. But his father was cold and reserved and dignified. The boy was scared stiff of him. About the only fun Reggie had with his father was when they went to soccer games together.

Years ago, Stanley Dwight had played the trumpet in a dance band. He had a great love for music which was inherited by his son. Little Reg began taking piano lessons when he was four. He was very nearly a musical genius. When Reg learned how to play some simple Chopin, his father said: "I'm proud of you."

Music became the most important thing in Reg Dwights life.

When Reg was only 11, he won a fellowship at the famous Royal Academy of Music. There he studied the classics. But his favorite music wasn't Chopin or Bach. It was rock'n'roll! Reg had bitter arguments with his father whenever he tried to play pop music.

Reg Dwight's teenage years were a time of great unhappiness. When he was 14, his parents were divorced. Reg lived with his mother, but his father still took an interest in him. Stanley was afraid that playing rock music would make a "wild boy" out of his son.

Sheila knew better. When she listened to Reg composing new versions of "Rock Around the Clock," she knew that he had a special talent for this kind of music. She allowed him to take a job playing piano in a nearby hotel. When he was 17, she let him drop out of school to become a full-time musician in a rhythm-and-blues band.

Young Reg Dwight was short, fat, and shy. But he loved playing piano in the band, Bluesology. He stuck with the outfit from 1964 until 1967. During that time, Bluesology became famous in a small way. Its lead singer was Long John Baldry, who had a hit record, "Let the Heartaches Begin." The sax player with the band was named Elton Dean.

But Reg Dwight became impatient after several years with Bluesology. It seemed that he would be nothing but a backup man with them. And he wanted something better. He wanted to write songs himself.

One day, Reg noticed a record-company ad that invited new talent to audition. He went to London to try his luck. But it was no sale. One good thing did happen to Reg as a result of that audition, however. A kindly recording executive gave Reg a sheaf of lyrics from a chicken-farmer in Lincolnshire.

"Maybe you can put this guy's stuff to music," he suggested.

Reg took the lyrics home with him. He decided that he liked them. He composed music to fit them and mailed them to the chicken-farmer, whose name was Bernie Taupin. For some time, the two wrote back and forth to each other. Finally they met and discovered that they were a natural song-writing team.

Reg worked off and on with Bluesology and also had a job as an errand boy in a record store. In his spare time, he wrote songs with Bernie. But at first, none of the songs were much good.

Elton

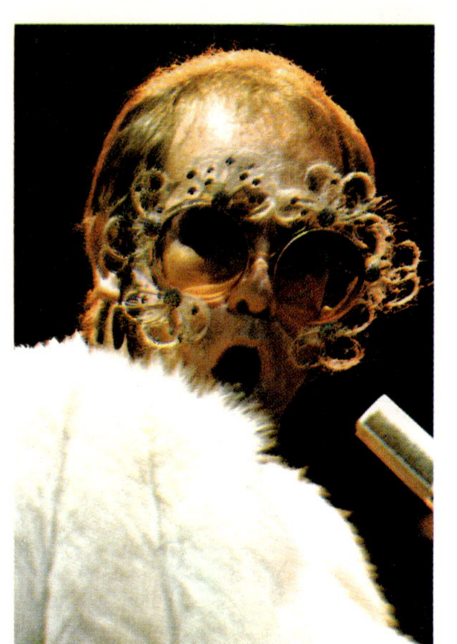

Reg had always been very shy around girls. Then he met Linda while he was playing a gig with Bluesology. She was 6 feet 2 inches tall. (Reg was 5-foot-8.) She came on very strong and Reg decided he was in love. He proposed marriage to Linda and she accepted. But before the wedding could come off, Linda broke up with Reg.

He was desolate. There seemed to be no reason to go on. He wanted to give up. But with the help of his friends, he decided to go on living. Life was too precious to be sacrificed for a broken heart.

Elton and Bernie got a contract writing songs for the Dick James Music Company. They finally had a hit, "Lady Samantha." Dick James told them that they should be recording their own stuff — not just writing for other people. It seemed like a good idea.

Reg Dwight decided he would take a new name. He combined the first names of Long John Baldry and Elton Dean from the Bluesology band and came up with **Elton John.**

It took three years — from 1967 until 1970 — for Elton John to find success. He and Bernie worked together, writing songs and presenting them before audiences in night clubs. First they played small places in Scotland. Sometimes it was very cold there and Elton jumped around the piano as he played — to keep warm! The jumping became part of the act.

Elton began to wear striking clothes. He studded his suits with tiny mirrors. Audiences liked that. Elton wasn't thin and romantic-looking like some other rock singers. So he had to find another gimmick that would make people remember him. The costumes and the mad stage antics served the purpose.

But all the foolery in the world won't draw audiences to a dull performer. Elton John had more than gimmicks going for him. His tunes and Bernie's lyrics were interesting and full of melody. He cut his first album, **"Empty Sky,"** in 1969.

American promoters decided to send Elton on a tour of the U.S.A. He did turnaway business at a famous club in Los Angeles in 1970 — and the road to superstardom began to open ahead of him.

Later in 1970, Elton sang at Fillmore East in New York. The concert was a huge success. One of Elton's songs, **"Your Song,"** became Number 1 in America. His album, **"Elton John,"** moved onto the chart in 1970 and stayed there until it won a gold record.

Then came other hit albums — **"Tumbleweed Connection,"** **"11-17-70,"** **"Friends,"** and **"Madman Across the Water."**

Tired out from the grind of endless concerts, Elton, Bernie, and their musicians took a breather. They spent some weeks in a French chateau — but they didn't really rest! Instead, they came up with a new album, **"Honky Chateau."** The songs in it were easier, happier. It was one of Elton's favorite efforts, earning him a platinum disc in 1972.

Elton John singles swamped American rock music stations. Among his hits were **"Honky Cat,"** **"Levon,"** **"Rocket Man,"** and **"Tiny Dancer."**

ELTON JOH
GOLD DISC
PRESENTATION

The year 1973 saw him bring out **"Don't Shoot Me, I'm Only the Piano Player"** and **"Goodbye Yellow Brick Road."** The title song of the latter became his best-known single hit.

People flocked to his concerts as he traveled all over the world. All kinds of fans came — young, old, straight, hip, rich, poor. He had songs for all of them. His hard rock numbers such as **"Burn Down the Mission"** and **"Crocodile Rock"** infected everyone with their excitement. More wistful numbers such as **"Don't Let the Sun Go Down on Me"** inspired audiences to light matches and hold them up in sympathy.

Some critics attacked Elton for his show biz gimmicks and the sentimentality of some of Bernie's lyrics. But what was wrong with sentiment? If you didn't feel life, what good was it?

Elton's 1975 Album, **"Captain Fantastic and the Brown Dirt Cowboy,"** was the story of the struggle he and Bernie had endured making it to the top. Its hit single, **"Someone Saved My Life,"** was all the more touching because it was true.

Elton's style became more and more outrageous as his popularity grew. As he sang, the stage would billow colored smoke. Birds, bubbles, balloons and butterflies floated around him. But his "glitter rock" staging was never shocking or ugly. It was good-humored, tongue-in-cheek. Elton was inviting the audience to laugh as well as listen to his songs.

In the rock movie **Tommy,** Elton played a singer called the Pinball Wizard. He wore stilts and huge shoes that made him 9 feet tall. How did it feel? "I got dizzy," he admitted. But he kept the giant boots in a place of honor in his rec room — along with his 10 gold and platinum albums and his 8 gold singles.

When he became rich and famous, he was able to do something else he had long dreamed of. He became a director of the Watford Hornets — the soccer team he and his father had cheered so long for. His happiest moments are spent practicing with the team.

He has threatened to "tone down his image" to a less frenzied pitch. But he hasn't done it yet. And a lot of fans hope he never will.

Dodgers
1

Stevie Wonder

Wonder is his name. And he is a wonder, for sure.

He's black, blind, and brilliant. He was a kid genius. He nearly died in a horrible accident. He's had not just one great career, but two. And he may add a few more onto that if the spirit moves him!

You can't label him as a soul singer. You can't label him as a rock or pop star. He's all of these and a lot more. People call him a legend. But he's not your ordinary dime-a-dozen super star. He's a man who sees beautiful things inside his mind — then brings them out for the wonderment of others.

He was born in 1950 in Saginaw, Michigan, the third of six children. And from the very beginning, little Steveland Morris was blind. Since he had never used his eyes, he didn't miss them. He was a happy child who first made music by banging spoons in time to a radio tune when he was two years old.

He didn't even know he was different from other kids until he was about four. Then his mother would scold him for stepping in dog messes in the back yard. "You'll just have to try and stay in one place, Stevie," she said. "You're not the same as the others."

Stevie's mother fretted about his blindness and prayed that he would be able to see. But Stevie said to her: "Mama, I'm happy being blind. It's just something God gave me."

When Stevie was very small, the family moved to the large city of Detroit. They lived in a housing project. Stevie's father didn't spend much time at home and his mother had to raise the children by herself. Sometimes they were so poor they had to steal coal from a loading dock to keep warm in the winter.

With the help of sighted friends, Stevie was able to wander all over the neighborhood. He learned to climb trees and was even able to ride a bicycle with one of his brothers steering from behind.

But the thing he loved best was music. Even when he was a tiny boy, he could beat out musical tempo. Once, at an outdoor band concert, the drummer let little Stevie sit on his lap and play a real drum. People clapped and threw coins when the little blind boy finished.

His uncle gave him a tiny harmonica when Stevie was four. He learned to play the toy — then got a larger harmonica and mastered it, too.

He was always visiting a neighbor lady who had a piano in her apartment. When the lady moved, she left the piano for Stevie. It was the best present he ever had — one that would shape the course of his whole life.

One Christmas, he got a real drum at a Lions Club party for blind children. He learned to play the bongos, too. All the kids in the neighborhood would come to hear little Stevie play.

When he was about eight, his father and mother separated. Stevie got to visit with his father from time to time. Nevertheless, he missed his father. And when he was 10, he wrote his first song, "Lonely Boy."

One of Stevie's friends introduced him to Ronnie White. Ronnie belonged to a group called the Miracles. They recorded on the Motown label. Impressed with the little boy's music, Ronnie took him down to the studio one day. Stevie was in heaven! All those instruments! He tried to play them all. The people at Motown really became attached to little Stevie. They let him hang around after school. He even played along with adult musicians.

Clarence Paul, a conductor at Motown, took Stevie in hand. The 10-year-old was given a contract and a new name. He became Little Stevie Wonder.

When Stevie was 12, he had his first big hit, "Fingertips." He sang and played the harmonica, accompanied by a big band. One critic said: "His raw, joyous harmonica jumps out of the disc like sparks from a welding torch."

The song was issued in an album, "12 Year Old Genius." The album became a best-seller and "Fingertips" earned a gold disc.

Stevie became so famous that he was mobbed when he attended the Detroit Public School. So he transfered to Michigan School for the Blind at Lansing. This school arranged special lessons for him. He was able to keep up his schoolwork even when he went on tour to give concerts.

The Motown people opened a whole new world to Little Stevie Wonder. They acted like a family and watched over him. Part of the money he earned went to his mother to help support the family. Most went into a trust fund that Stevie would get when he was 21 years old. All Stevie got was an allowance of $2.50.

He had hit after hit. Among his important singles were "Signed, Sealed, and Delivered," "My Cherie Amour," "Uptight," "For Once in My Life," and "I Was Made to Love Her." Most of these weren't soul music at all. They were middle-of-the-road pop tunes that were purchased by both black and white buyers, and by older people as well as young.

Stevie Wonder just loved to perform. Sometimes, when a show was over, Clarence Paul had to pick him up and haul him off the stage before he would quit playing!

He had one problem as a performer. Like many blind people, he had excess energy. This led him to a nervous habit (called a "blindism") of moving his head jerkily in time to the music. The habit made some people uneasy. They wondered if Stevie used drugs. He didn't, though. He said: "If I were high on drugs it would destroy the character of my music. I'd be tripping out on myself instead of concentrating on the songs in my mind."

When Stevie was 21, in 1971, all the money that had been held back was given to him. He decided to strike out on his own. He moved out of his family's home in Detroit and went to New York. He married Syreeta Wright, who had been a secretary at Motown.

Stevie spent a quarter of a million dollars producing his new record, "Music of My Mind." It was a remarkable effort that earned a gold award. In it, Stevie not only sang, but also played most of the instruments. They were recorded one at a time and then blended together electronically into a full orchestra effect. He wrote and arranged all the music himself. Much of it was played on a Moog synthesizer, allowing him to experiment with unusual sounds.

He said: "I feel the Moog gives a way to directly express what comes from your mind." The music was about as far from middle-of-the-road as you could get. Stevie didn't intend for the album to become a popular success. But it was, all the same.

"Little" Stevie Wonder had faded quietly away. In his place was a 6-foot young man, wise beyond his years. He had made the tough jump from child stardom to adult stardom. Not many performers have been so lucky.

Stevie with good friend Roberta Flack

In 1972 he had a million-copy album, **"Talking Book."** Three of his singles topped the charts — **"Superstition," "Super Woman,"** and the blockbuster **"You Are the Sunshine of My Life."**

His 14th album, "Innervisions," came out in June 1973. It contained not only music, but also ideas. Stevie sang about himself in relation to the world in "Living for the City" and "Visions." The first was about the tragedy of urban ghettos. The second song dreamed of a better world where all people were friendly — and wondered whether such a dream could ever become real.

Just two months after this album came out, Stevie Wonder lay close to death in a hospital. He had been riding in a car on a highway in North Carolina. A logging truck was ahead of them. Suddenly a chain snapped and a log came crashing through the windshield, striking Stevie in the forehead.

He was in a coma for a week, not moving, nearly dead. One of his grief-stricken friends leaned over his bed and softly sang **"Higher Ground."** It was a hymnlike song from his latest album telling of God's saving power.

Slowly, Stevie's fingers began to move in time with the music. He was going to recover. Later on, "Higher Ground," with its message about being glad that God let him "try it again," became a hit single.

Some months later, Stevie felt much better. His friend, Elton John, invited him to come to Boston for a concert that Elton was giving. Stevie traveled there on Elton's private plane. He listened from backstage while Elton brought down the house.

After the first encore, Elton had something to say to the 18,000 people who packed Boston Gardens. "A friend of mine is here tonight. He was badly hurt in an accident some time ago . . . "

Elton never got to finish his speech. Everybody knew who he was talking about. The place erupted with applause as Stevie Wonder came out. He and Elton played **"Honky Tonk Woman"** together. Then Stevie did a solo of his great hit, **"Superstition."**

The cheering throng in Boston knew that Stevie Wonder was back — and he was better than ever.

By March 1974, Stevie had won five Grammy Awards — for best pop vocalist **"You Are the Sunshine"**; for best rhythm-and-blues vocalist **"Superstition"**; for writing the best R&B song **"Superstition"** again; for the best-engineered non-classical album **"Innervisions"**; and for album of the year **"Innervisions"**.

Stevie and then wife Syreeta decided to go their separate ways and soon after Stevie met Yolanda Simmons. In April 1975, Stevie and Yolanda became the parents of a baby girl named Aisha.

Just a month earlier, Stevie had won five more Grammies. This time the featured album was **"Fulfillingness' First Finale,"** and the singles were **"Boogie On Reggae Woman"** and **"Living for the City."**

And a few weeks after Aisha's birth, Stevie was honored at Washington's annual Human Kindness Day. Some 50,000 fans gathered on the grounds of the Washington Monument to salute him and hear him sing.

Stevie Wonder donated money and time to worthy causes such as the Stevie Wonder Home for Blind and Retarded Children. He served as a trustee of Shaw University in Raleigh, N.C. and set up scholarships for blind students

Then, after months of tours, he settled down in 1976 to work on musical projects such as his unusual double album, **"Songs in the Key of Life,"** and his hit single, **"Don't You Worry 'Bout a Thing."** Almost all of his music symbolizes his deep inner belief in the goodness of mankind.

"When I look at an audience," Stevie says, tapping his black glasses, "all I see are beautiful people."

John Denver

Now everybody who knows pop music knows his name. He's a multi-millionaire. A 23-piece orchestra backs up his "simple" songs of the outdoors. But it wasn't always like that.

John Denver says: "I can remember going to Cedar Rapids, Iowa and getting there when it was 10 below zero. I had to load five boxes of sound equipment on a truck myself and drive it to the gym where I was scheduled to perform. Wouldn't you know — I left my gloves at home. But I loaded the stuff, drove to the school, got some people to help unload and set it up. Then there was time to take a shower, get tuned up and all, and do a 2-1/2 hour show."

Then it was back to his home in Edina, Minnesota. His wife, Annie, was working on her degree in music education whiie John picked up singing jobs here and there. Things were tough. But John Denver never thought of quitting.

"I could see that the audience liked me," he says. "And I knew that I never went out in front of 24 people and did any less of a show than I did in front of 250 people. I had found something very important. I'd found out what worked for me and I was determined to keep on doing it."

Determined. That's the word for John Denver. He doesn't want to do a thing unless he feels that it's right. He doesn't want to sing unless he can sing about things he believes in.

You know he takes his songs seriously. So you have to listen. And likely as not, you'll find yourself believing in the songs yourself!

He sings about things that are real. He has experienced the glory of **"Rocky Mountain High."** He admires the good work done by Captain Cousteau and the men of **"Calypso."** You know John is a happy man when he sings **"Sunshine,"** and you know he loves his wife when he sings **"Annie's Song."**

He sings of a simple life-style in **"Take Me Home, Country Roads."** He mourns the people trapped in ugly cities when he and Olivia Newton-John combine talents in the haunting **"Fly Away."**

Many show business peole had unhappy childhoods. But this was not true of John Denver. He was born in 1943 on the last day of the year in Roswell, New Mexico. His real name is Henry John Deutschendorf, Jr.

His father was a career Air Force pilot who held three world records in military aviation. Like many service families, the Deutschendorfs traveled a lot. They lived near Air Force bases in Arizona, Oklahoma, Japan, and Alabama.

John was rather small and shy. Every time the family moved, he would have to make new friends all over again. His grandmother gave him an old guitar when he was in the seventh grade. He learned to play and sing — and the guitar became his key to friendship.

One of John's first press shots

"All of a sudden people would know me," he remembers. "After I played the guitar, kids would say hello in the halls at school. Music is what opened the door for me."

The family moved to Fort Worth, Texas, when John was 13. He went to high school there and became known for his excellent guitar playing. By then he had not only his grandma's old guitar, (famed in his song **"This Old Guitar"**) but also an electric instrument with an amp.

It was the time of the folk-song craze. John felt right at home with that kind of music. He imitated the sound of the Kingston Trio and also tried playing rock in the style of the Everly Brothers.

When he was a senior in high school, he rebelled against his parents and ran away to California. But he soon ran out of money and called his Dad, who came and brought him home. The family disagreement was patched up and John finished school.

John entered Texas Tech at Lubbock to study architecture. He did fairly well at college for two years. At the same time, he kept up with his music. He admired the work of the Chad Mitchell Trio, Joan Baez, Peter, Paul and Mary, and the New Christy Minstrels.

Playing guitar and singing meant a lot more to John than his studies. His grades began to slump during his third year in college. Finally, in 1964, he wrote to his parents and told them he wanted to quit.

John remembers: "They did what I think is the greatest thing any parents could do for their children. They didn't approve of my decision, but they gave me the space to go." Henry and Erma Deutschendorf sent their son $200 to help get him started in his new music career.

John took the money and went to California. He played odd gigs at college hootenannies and also worked as a draftsman to keep from starving. The following year, he got a job at Ledbetter's folk club where Randy Sparks helped him find a style of his own.

A man from a record company came by and heard John. He suggested that the young guitarist do a demo record. "But you'll have to change your name," he said. "Deutschendorf is too long and too hard to spell."

John was proud of his name and reluctant to change. But he finally agreed to one of the names the record producer suggested. His new name became **"John Denver."** The city of Denver, Colorado seemed to embody the high country that John loved.

Unfortunately, the demo record never amounted to anything. But not long after that, John did get his big break. He auditioned as a replacement for the famed Chad Mitchell, who was leaving the trio he had founded. And John Denver was picked over 300 others to become a singer in the New Mitchell Trio, beginning in 1965. He would continue with the Trio for the next three years.

John and Annie on their wedding day

During the first season with the Mitchell Trio, John played a gig at Gustavus Adolphus College in Minnesota. He saw a girl in a college show there and fell in love with her at first sight. But he was too shy even to ask her name!

A whole year later, the Trio came to Minnesota again. John worked up his courage and got the phone number of the girl, whose name was Ann-Marie Martell. He invited her to his concert. She came. He invited her to another concert — and she came again.

Whenever he could get away from the Trio, John visited Annie in Minnesota. He was the guest of the Martell family during Christmas 1966. He followed Annie and her college ski club to Aspen, Colorado, early the next year.

The beauty of the snowy mountains beneath the blue sky overwhelmed John. This was his country! And Annie was his girl.

They were married in June 1967 in her home town of St. Peter, Minnesota.

It wasn't all roses during those early days of marriage. John really had to scratch around to get bookings for the Mitchell Trio. The folk music fad was dying and hard rock was the coming thing.

The records made by the new Trio did not sell. Their college tours made less and less money. The two original men dropped out and were replaced — making a whole new group. Their music was good, but they had lost their audience.

Finally, in 1969, John Denver decided to go it alone. He played at a club named the Leather Jug in Snowmass, Colorado, near Aspen. The skiers liked John and he polished his act to their admiring applause. He wrote a song, "Aspenglow," that celebrated the snowy slopes and the people who skied them.

Meanwhile, another song of John's was gaining fame. He had first recorded **"Leaving on a Jet Plane"** in 1967 on a limited-edition album given only to his friends. Peter, Paul and Mary, a famous folk trio, liked the song and recorded it themselves.

It became a huge hit in 1969, earning a gold record. John, the composer of the song, was able to cash in on its fame and make a solo album, **"Rhymes & Reasons,"** with a big company, RCA.

In 1970 he cut two more albums, **"Take Me to Tomorrow"** and **"Whose Garden Was This."** They weren't exactly best-sellers, but they did gain John a devoted following. His concerts attracted large audiences. He and Annie were able to move from Minnesota to the place they both loved best — Aspen, Colorado.

Count Basie, John Denver and Frank Sinatra swing on one of John's TV specials

John appeared on television and at folk festivals. He became modestly famous and prosperous. Two of his friends, Bill and Taffy Danoff, showed him a song they had been unable to finish. John liked it and helped write the rest of the song. He sang it and included it in his 1971 album, "Poems, Prayers, and Promises."

The song was a smash — **"Take Me Home, Country Roads."** It earned a gold disc as a single, and so did John's album.

John Denver was launched toward super stardom. His next two albums, **"Aerie"** and **"Rocky Mountain**

High," were quickly turned to gold. He became famous as the troubadour of unspoiled nature. All over the United States, people were looking at the outdoors and wondering how it could be saved from the spoilers. John Denver's songs were part of the environmental movement.

His concerts were without gimmicks. He often sang against projected backgrounds of mountain scenery. He was clean and straight and happy and popular with a wide audience. Teens through grandparents — they all enjoyed John Denver.

He says of his audiences: "You can watch them as I sing a song like **'Sunshine.'** They're all right there with it. But you've got to know they're getting different pictures from it."

Different pictures, yes. But also pictures that are similar. Pictures of a man with a message of joy and hope. Pictures of a man who loves the beauty of nature and wants others to join him in that love.

People wonder if John Denver is too good to be true. Does he live the way he sings?

It's hard to be humble when you're a millionaire. And it's hard to live quietly when people are clamoring for concerts, TV shows, movies, and recording sessions.

But within his limits, John Denver does live the life he sings about. He and Annie and their little son, Zach, spend as much time as possible in a home hidden away in the Colorado mountains. They avoid the limelight.

"I've been very fortunate," John says. "I wanted to sing for people and I wanted to live in Colorado. And I've been able to do it. I've been kind of on a path that's brought me here. I am what I've always wanted to be. I'm gonna go on singing as long as there's an audience that wants to hear me."